Independence Day

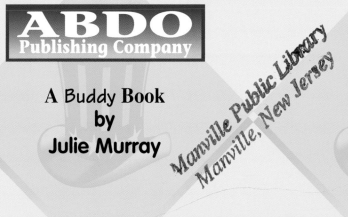

ABDO
Publishing Company

A Buddy Book
by
Julie Murray

Visit us at
www.abdopub.com

Published by ABDO Publishing Company, 4940 Viking Drive, Edina, Minnesota 55435.

Printed in the United States.

Edited by: Sarah Tieck
Contributing Editor: Michael P. Goecke
Graphic Design: Denise Esner
Image Research: Deborah Coldiron, Maria Hosley
Photographs: Comstock, Corbis, Eyewire, North Wind Archives, Photospin

Library of Congress Cataloging-in-Publication Data

Murray, Julie, 1969-
  Independence Day / Julie Murray.
      p. cm. — (Holidays)
  Summary: An introduction to the Fourth of July holiday, including its history and the various ways in which it has been celebrated.
  Includes bibliographical references (p.) and index.
  Contents: Independence Day — The story of independence — Declaration of Independence — Spreading the news — Early celebrations — 100 years later — 200 years later — Symbols of independence.
  ISBN 1-59197-588-3
      1. Fourth of July—Juvenile literature. 2. Fourth of July celebrations—Juvenile literature.
  [1. Fourth of July. 2. Holidays.] I. Title.

E286.A14 2005
394.2634—dc22
                                                                2003055830

Table of Contents

What Is Independence Day?

Independence Day is America's birthday. This **holiday** is on July 4 each year. It is sometimes called the Fourth of July. Many Americans celebrate with parades, fireworks, picnics, and **patriotic** songs.

Americans celebrate Independence Day at the nation's capitol.

The Fourth Of July Story

In the 1770s, America was made up of 13 **colonies**. King George III was the King of England. He ruled the colonies and made all their laws. Many people wanted to be free from the laws and rules of England.

King George III was the ruler of England.

England and the 13 **colonies** went to war over independence in 1775. This was called the Revolutionary War. Famous men such as George Washington, John Adams, and Thomas Jefferson led the fight for freedom.

In 1776, members of the Second Continental Congress made plans to break away from England. They met at the State House in Philadelphia. They chose Thomas Jefferson to write America's Declaration of Independence. John Adams, Benjamin Franklin, Robert Livingston, and Roger Sherman helped him write it.

Thomas Jefferson, Benjamin Franklin, Robert Livingston, John Adams, and Roger Sherman in 1776.

The Declaration of Independence

Many members of the Congress signed the Declaration of Independence on July 4, 1776. This piece of paper said the **colonies** were free and independent from England. Now, the 13 colonies were called the United States of America.

Fifty-six people disobeyed King George III by signing their names. This was against the law. If the United States lost the Revolutionary War, the men who signed would be punished. Their lives were in danger.

July 8, 1776, was an important day in America. The Liberty Bell rang and people gathered at the State House in Philadelphia. Colonel John Nixon read the Declaration of Independence to everyone there. Thousands of people celebrated.

The first reading of the Declaration of Independence was held in Philadelphia.

In 1776, people had to hand deliver messages to one another. Men on horses took copies of the Declaration of Independence to people all over the 13 **colonies**.

The Revolutionary War was not over, but people celebrated. This was the first step toward independence from England. Americans burned **symbols** of England in huge bonfires, watched soldiers march in parades, and fired cannons.

Words Of The Declaration Of Independence

The Declaration of Independence was written in 1776.

Thomas Jefferson wrote the Declaration of Independence in 1776. Its words are famous. It said, "all men are created equal." It also stated that each person has a right to "Life, Liberty, and the pursuit of Happiness." This says that all **citizens** have the same rights.

This piece of paper also said the **colonies** were free from England's laws. Thomas Jefferson explained the reasons why. The Declaration of Independence was approved by the Congress on July 4, 1776.

The First Independence Day

One year later on July 4, 1777, people gathered in Philadelphia to celebrate freedom. Philadelphia had the first Independence Day. This was a time of confusion. The United States and England were still at war. The Revolutionary War did not officially end until 1783. Still, people celebrated their new country's birthday.

Americans knock down a statue of King George III in 1776 to celebrate independence.

On July 4, 1777, bells chimed. Ships fired 13 shots in honor of the 13 **colonies**. Soldiers marched in parades through the streets. Fireworks and bonfires lit up the night skies. People lit candles in their windows to show they were **patriotic**. There was even a special dinner.

Becoming A National Tradition

Soon, other cities around the United States had celebrations on July 4. Each year important people gave speeches about freedom. Marching bands played songs like "Yankee Doodle."

The centennial Fourth of July celebration in 1876.

The **centennial** of America's independence was in 1876. Celebrations were held all over the country. Celebrations lasted well into the night with fireworks, music, and cheering.

America's **bicentennial** happened in 1976. People across the United States celebrated freedom. Bells rang. President Gerald Ford gave a speech. There were gun salutes and ship parades. Fireworks lit up the night skies.

Symbols Of Independence

The Flag

    The flag **symbolizes** the United States of America. The flag's seven red stripes and six white stripes stand for the original 13 **colonies**. Fifty white stars represent 50 states. Many people fly their flag on the Fourth of July and other special occasions.

The Liberty Bell

The Liberty Bell has become a **symbol** of freedom. The word "liberty" means to be free. The Liberty Bell is a part of American history. For this reason, people honor it.

The Statue of Liberty

The Statue of Liberty is in New York City on Liberty Island. It was a gift from France to celebrate America's independence from England. Millions of **immigrants** saw the Statue of Liberty when they first came to America.

Celebrations Today

Today, Americans celebrate Independence Day. Many people honor the holiday in the same ways they did more than 225 years ago.

People celebrate Independence Day with fireworks.

The American flag is a symbol of freedom. It is often seen on Independence Day.

Independence Day is a time of fun and celebration for many families. Many cities host celebrations. **Customs** include parades, fireworks, and barbecues.

Many people fly the flag and listen to marching bands play songs like "Yankee Doodle." Some families decorate with red, white, and blue colors. Others play games or spend the day at beaches, parks, or lakes.

Independence Day is about the freedoms of the United States of America.

Important Words

bicentennial 200-year anniversary.

centennial 100-year anniversary.

citizen a member of a city or town.

colonies the 13 original states.

custom a practice that has been around a long time. Fireworks are a custom of Independence Day.

holiday a special time for celebration.

immigrant someone who moves from a different country.

patriotic loyalty to a country.

symbol an object or mark that stands for an idea.

Web Sites

To learn more about Independence Day, visit ABDO Publishing Company on the World Wide Web. Web site links about Independence Day are featured on our Book Links page. These links are routinely monitored and updated to provide the most current information available.

www.abdopub.com

Index